An Endless Namaste

SUSAN TELFORD

Poems of Awakening

For Dennis

With Endless Love

Table of Contents

Introduction 1

The Body Knows 3

Down Among The Broken Ones 7

There Is Nothing Wrong 11

Fierce Grace 15

Fierce Grace 2 21

Song Of The Mother 25

The River Of Joy 29

Be A Rose 35

God Lives Here.. 39

My Teacher, The Tree 43

Red 47

I Choose Joy 49

Non-Doing.. 53

Let Go 55

Stay Home.. 59

Unchanging 63

Cathedral 67

Be Still 71

Not Even That... 77

My True Name 79

I Am 81

The Deep Peace Of Surrender 87

Pilgrimage.. 91

Invincible Summer 95

Flow 97

Be 101

Ctrl-Alt-Delete 103

Dance 107

Surrender... 109

Swaddled By Grace 111

Freedom 113

There Is Only One 119

Fresh News 123

Beyond All Thought 127

Silence 129

Only God 131

Everything Is.. 135

A Dance Of Love 137

The Sanctuary Of Now...................................... 139

Don't Forget To Laugh!..................................... 141

I Am That I Am.. 143

An Endless Namaste 145

Introduction

Writing poetry was never a part of my life, until it all fell apart in 2016.

I went from working crazy hours in a busy high school as a Maths teacher to lying in bed staring out of the window, too exhausted even to read.

But in 2017, a strange thing started to happen. As I recovered from the burnout that ended my teaching career, I began to write in my journal, trying to make sense of what had happened to me and why, poems started to appear on the page.

At first, I did not understand what was happening, I worried that I was developing a mental illness. I came to see that what was happening was a spiritual awakening and the poems were like messengers from the Divine.

They led me, poem by poem, back to health, and as I continued to follow these poetic breadcrumbs, they led me to a new career as a coach and spiritual mentor, to managing a large global spiritual community, becoming a podcast host and being ordained as an interfaith minister.

They guided me to see more and more clearly the truth of who I am and to let go of **everything** that had previously defined me.

I offer these poems of awakening to you, with the prayer that by reading them (or listening by clicking on each poem's title), you will have a spark of recognition your true nature.

Namaste!

Susan

The Body Knows

The body knows

The lies you tell

The headache blooms

Where love is blocked

The wrong path

Knots your stomach

With the nausea of self-abandonment

The fear of being seen

Your precious life energy

Exchanged for acceptance.

You push on

Too busy to notice

The birds gliding effortlessly through the sky

The flower buds gently opening

The return of the spring sun

These masters showing the way home.

You push down the truth emerging

Still trying to be good

Forgetting your own innate perfection.

There is nowhere to get to

Nothing to strive for

Everything is a gift you rejected over and over

Until now.

Down Among The Broken Ones

Come down among the broken ones
Who gave their hearts away
Who tried to help, who tried to love
All those who came their way.

Come down among the lost ones
Whose way of being died
Who gave their all, till all was gone
And darkness lit their way.

Come down among the lonely ones
Who tried so hard to please
Who noticed when in need themselves
That all had gone away.

Come down, my love, and don't be scared

For nothing is as it seems

Here in the depths of loneliness

Is the medicine you need.

Come down and feel your beating heart

The space between your thoughts

Cradle your fragile, tender soul

And notice what you are.

The life you knew is over

Shed tears for all that's lost

Then notice too the birds and trees

You were once too blind to see

You had to lose the life you had

It hurts, I know, but soon

You will awaken to reality

The light of who you are

There Is Nothing Wrong

Can you see it, my love?

You are beginning to wake up.

Can you see what we have done together?

You are ready to trust.

Can you see the perfection

of all the things you fought so hard against?

The pain of losing it all, the loneliness of chronic illness,

the stripping away of all you thought defined you.

You are beyond definitions.

The joy when the mind agreed that it was right,

the pain from thinking things have gone wrong.

There is nothing wrong.

Nothing can ever go wrong in this perfection.

You are standing, now, on the threshold,

knowing that your arrival here is inevitable.

In the quietness of your mind,

in this vast still place where you belong,

from which you came and to which you return,

you know the truth.

There is nothing wrong.

I will whisper it, in songs of love.

I will shout it, through screams of pain.

There is nothing wrong.

The heart slows, the mind stills, the eyes open,

blinking in this new reality, as old as time.

Trust all that comes,

love everything that arises as though you chose it.

Because you did.

Fierce Grace

Fierce Grace swept into your life

Destroying all your carefully made plans.

You loved your achievements.

You thought your intentions were pure.

But you came here to BE LOVE

Let go, my love, into the abyss of exhaustion.

Let go into the realm of everything apparently gone wrong

Let go of who you thought you were

Who you were told you are

And remember who you really are

Deep in that abyss, I will meet you

Swirling around you

with my fierce, love-soaked grace.

Whisper my words

Make them your constant prayer

There is nothing wrong, there is nothing wrong, there is nothing wrong.

Soothe your mind as it barks its objections

Soothe your weary heart

Cradle yourself as your own beloved child.

Rest.

Feel.

Cry.

Listen.

Nothing to do, nowhere to go

Nothing to be

Except who you are

In truth

Fierce Grace is emptying you

Of all your striving

This fierce Grace

Manifested in you,

Manifested as you

Will crack you open

That is how the light gets out.

Fierce Grace 2

Do not be afraid of the fierceness of Grace

As she razes your house to the ground

She comes to reveal your original face

As you blink back tears in this strange, new place

She will not leave you where you were found

Do not be afraid of the fierceness of Grace.

She comes to teach life is not a race

No winners or losers on this holy ground

She comes to reveal your original face.

She breaks you down, she slows your pace

Frees you where you were bound

Do not be afraid of the fierceness of Grace.

And in Her silence, you will find the space

Where peace and joy abound

She comes to reveal your original face.

Until, at last, there is no trace

No you, no Her, newfound

Do not be afraid of the fierceness of Grace

She came to reveal your original face.

Song Of The Mother

Go slowly

Nestle under my wings

Breathe my breath

Sing my song

Love whatever is arising.

All pain and sorrow

Are your lost children

Re-emerging

To be loved at last.

You are the one

They have waited for

To love them.

Embrace those shut-out children

Banished from your heart

The lonely one

The angry one

The misunderstood one

The isolated one

The rejected one

The girl with the light in her eyes

Who hid herself away.

Each one steps forward now

Brave enough now

To surrender

To your loving embrace.

Greet them all

Your own beloved children

Braid their hair

Sing them songs of love.

Oh my darlings

You are home

Welcome at last

Just as you are.

The River Of Joy

Step into the river

Of love-soaked joy

It will carry you home

Silence monkey-mind objections

Loosen tight fingers of control

I gave you Eden

Accept my gift

Stop, now

Watch the trees

Leaves and branches moved by Love

Watch the rise and fall of your chest

Breathed by Love

Watch the actions of your body

Moved by Joy

Listen, now

The birdsong

Purring cat, rustling paper

Everything, here, now

For your pleasure

Taste, now

The bounty of nature

Sweet fruit, Divine nectar

For you, my love, for you.

Open all your windows

Smell salt sea air

Incense of the gods

Let me blow through you.

Let me touch you, now

Feel the light filled bursts of joy

Erupting in your cells

I left my breadcrumbs

In the last place you thought to look

See them, now

Where they always were

Here, now

Inside, outside

No difference.

Step into the river

Of love-soaked joy

It will carry you home.

Be A Rose

I prayed

"Make me a vessel of the Divine."

God laughed.

"That is like the rose asking me to make it a flower."

Does the rose need my assistance to become a flower?

Which good works must it do to attain flowerhood?

All the rose can do is bloom, at its appointed hour

Unashamed to be a rose

unafraid to show her beauty.

Being only what she is.

You want to be a vessel of my love?

You are already that.

Now, bloom where you are planted

Be the variety of rose

Only you can be

In your garden, among the other flowers.

Some will show their thorns

They are as beloved

As those who perfume the world.

Stop looking outside yourself

Stop striving

The end of suffering is here

Closer than your breath

Will you give up all worlds

But this, appearing now?

Give up the search

Give up your longing

Be a rose."

God Lives Here

Sticky orange scented fingers

A cloudless sky

Two shafts of light

God lives here

A dimly lit kitchen

A raging hurt boy-husband

Ugly tears, mind stopped in grief

God lives here

Sitting in meditation

Amid Tibetan Buddhist artefacts

Sunlight patch on wooden floor

God lives here

Lying in bed

Exhaustion and tears

The sunlight in the trees

God lives here

Raging against injustice

The mind wants to be right

The piercing light of nothing wrong

God lives here

The flea infested house

The mad scratch of itchy puppy

The jolt of plans gone wrong

God lives here

No journey to take

No plans to make

God lives here

Among it all.

My Teacher, The Tree

Autumn

No resistance to the shedding

The beauty in letting go

Winter

No resistance to the storms

The beauty of being blown

Spring

No resistance to the blooming

The beauty of new growth

Summer

No resistance to the fullness

The beauty of it all.

Later…..

Branches gone, stripped bare

Essence remains, still a tree

Nothing real is lost

Red

Cut me open

I bleed red

Passion, pain

It's all the same

Colour of love

Shade of desire

Flames of surrender

On my funeral pyre

Sunsets and lava

Tastes of Divine

I claim this redness

All that IS, mine.

I Choose Joy

A thousand times a day

I squander joy

A thousand times a day

I argue

Giving what you say

What they do

Power

To veil the radiance

I am made of

A thousand times a day

I choose again

Remembering the ocean of bliss

In which I swim

No longer willing to pay

The ransom

The lie that I am not

Already free

I choose joy

A thousand times a day.

Non-Doing

Surrender the steel-trap mind

Become empty

Spacious

The witness

Life is living you

Love is breathing you

Mystery is moving you

Notice

No need to steer the ship

Lie back on the deck

And watch the sky!

Let Go

The time for effort has passed

Let go of the illusion that you are a seeker

progressing along a path to awakening.

Enter the place of spontaneity.

Relax into the posture of effortless acceptance.

The thinking mind cannot know anything of reality.

It cannot know what anything is for

or how all things work together for good

Let go completely

of the need to know,

to control, to fix, to understand.

Drown in the sea of unknowing,

where all things are left exactly as they are.

Let go of all thought of

I want this

I don't want that.

Who is this "I" who wants?

You were never that.

Sense the thrilling freedom

of loving all things exactly as they are.

Nothing to do

Nowhere to go

Just awareness being itSelf

Moving as It will.

Stay Home

Nothing exists but the Self

All things arise and dissolve within the Self

Find the Self which was never lost

And Be

Lay down your burdens

They were never yours to carry

Stay and rest

Where you have always dwelt

Give up your fake job

In the "make me happy squad"

Board the train

Of divine unemployment

Where you can relax

Until the next station appears

Stay home today

No need to scurry here and there

Searching for your Self

You are here, now, always

Stay home

And watch the comings and goings

From the unmoving

Unmoveable Love that you are

Unchanging

I am the unchanging One

Present

in the midst of change

I am the Unaffected One

Present

as the body weeps

I am the peaceful One

Present

in the midst of war

I am the joyful One

Present

as the heart breaks

I cradle my humanity

with the exquisite love

Of the Divine Mother

No denial

No bypass

No turning away

From what is

Just Being

The Love

that loves it all.

Cathedral

Slow Sunday stillness

Noticing

Eyes once used to straining forward

Content to rest

Here, now

Hot tea curling steam

Cat purring soft and low

Puppy damp from Sunday shower

Darts from room to room

Exuberant energy

Bubbling over

Cat regards her

Feline eyebrow raised as if to say

"Daft dog"

Candles glow

Air redolent with incense

"Mystic yoga" today

The scratch of pen on paper

Morning pages

The purple ink anchors of my life

Connecting me back to stillness

Always present

Often forgotten

Remembering again and again

Word by word by word

My handmade tether to Truth

Puppy worn out now

Joins us

Slow Sunday stillness

In the cathedral of my bed.

Be Still

You do not have to be good.

You do not have to constantly give

And worry

Until you fall exhausted in your bed

You do not have to hold

The weight of the world

On your shoulders

It is time to receive

It is time to replenish

It is time to turn within

To listen to the whispers of the voice

That has been trying to get your attention

That you were too busy for

Until now

Everything that happens is for your good.

Even if you cannot see it now

You are given daily bread

So follow the breadcrumbs appearing at your feet.

Hand over all your concerns

And in return receive

the gift of peace

the serenity of knowing

the next right action will be shown

You only have to ask

Be still

Know that everything you need is given

At the perfect time

Be still.

Be still.

You are perfectly guided, perfectly loved.

Trust.

Be still.

Receive

Rejoice.

Not Even That

The one who wanted to know

Knows nothing

The I that I thought I was

Quietly slips away

And not even that

The I who wanted to know

Never existed

All that remains

Is what is

Always here

Stillness

Joy

Love

I AM

And not even that

My True Name

Call me by my true name

Luminous Awareness

Pristine Presence

Silent Stillness

Aware Being

Joyful Existence

I AM

I AM

I AM

I Am

Although the winds may blow

You move in Me

Under My watchful eye

See My divine nature

Everywhere

Worship Me

As Source of All

Sing of My divine glory

See My face

Everywhere

I AM

The Alpha and the Omega

Your Father

Your Mother

Your Home

Your Refuge

Your One True Friend

Appearing

Everywhere

Meditate on Me

Make every breath

Your worship of Me

Give Me each aspect of your life

As an offering

Fill yourself with Me

Love Me

Serve Me

Worship Me

Everywhere

The Deep Peace Of Surrender

You STILL think you are Susan

Be STILL and know that I AM

See ONLY God

Want nothing

Enjoy everything

Dwell in the deep peace of surrender.

Dwell in the deep peace of surrender

Surrender to what is

Accept all things exactly as they are.

Dwell in the deep peace of surrender to *who* you are

Dwell in the deep peace of surrender to I AM

the true Self

Dwell in the deep peace of surrender of being breathed

Dwell in the deep peace of surrender of being moved

Dwell in the deep peace of surrender of your mind, your senses,
your emotions

Dwell in the deep peace of surrendering Susan

Stay in the still centre

Dwell in the deep peace of surrender

In this placeless place is perfect peace.

Pilgrimage

The river

Sun sparkles dancing

Smell of early morning

Chorus of the dawn

Welcoming me

Remind me I belong

Walking

A pilgrimage

To my Self

Nature arising

Moment by moment

Breath by breath

Step by step

Every step

Takes me closer

Every breath

Every birdsong

Every sparkling light

On the water

Speaks to me

Of God.

Invincible Summer

My heart is full of joy

Even in the depths of winter

While snow falls on illusory ground

The light of Spirit surrounds me

I AM that Light

No more need for protection

No more need for safety

I choose to bloom

In all weathers

In all seasons

In the joy of the eternal present

What Camus said is true

"I have discovered within me

An invincible summer"

Flow

Learn from the inner Teacher

With one-pointed awareness

Live rooted in the present

Aware of every step, every gesture, every movement

Flow with what Is

Surrender to the divine

Do not rush ahead

Love everything

It comes at its appointed time

Allow the process of purification

That will allow your mud to settle

And the water to clear

When this is accomplished

All decisions will make themselves

And all you feel is joy!

Be

Let go of every idea

Every plan

And surrender

You will be told

All you need to know

When you need to know it

Your job is to

Rest

Ask

Listen

Follow

Flow

Be present

Be available

Be still

Be

Ctrl-Alt-Delete

I do not know what anything is for.

Susan is being deleted.

All Susan's plans are being deleted.

Susan is being emptied

Divested

Simply resting at the centre

I wait

With no destination in view.

I come undone.

As I enter the space of non-action.

Not my will, but yours.

Nothing is impossible

I let go and let go and let go.

Rest

Trust

Just this

Just this

Just this.

Dance

Step into the ocean

Of pure potentiality

From the silent Presence

Of Being

Expressing its freedom through you

Come infinite worlds

Kaleidoscopes

Shifting

Dancing

Everything caused by everything

Lila

Allow yourself to be danced by God

Dance as God

Choose to let go

Into the arms of

The great Choreographer of All.

Surrender

Who is it who has a problem?

Surrender that.

Resign as the doer.

Step back and become like a window.

The light of reality will stream through you

Stop pretending to be in charge.

Trust that Life will move you.

Trust in Infinite Intelligence

Trust the Creative Power

The personality cannot understand this.

Don't even try.

Simply agree

To surrender

Follow guidance

Into the problem-free unknown.

Swaddled By Grace

Be still.

Be present

Be open

Be innocent

Be an open-mouthed baby bird

You are being fed

You are being led

Unfurl those tight fingers

Lay down the need to know

You are swaddled by Grace

Made of Light

Made to radiate

The Love that you are.

Freedom

Sitting in the garden

Contemplation

Tears stream

Broken open.

Tree beauty

Birdsong

Sunkissed skin

This peace

This beauty

Reflection of mind.

No grasping

No holding,

The witness

Of colours

Sounds

Flavours

Thoughts

I no longer want things to be a certain way.

I learned

All suffering is contained

in the word

SHOULD.

I have heard it a thousand times

Want nothing

Enjoy everything

Let go

Everything comes and goes

without your consent anyway

It is true

Rest in the freedom beyond letting go
No-one to let go and nothing to let go of.
This is your true nature
The paradox of being and non-being
A heart as open as the sky.

There Is Only One

There is only one

Not many

Not even two

Say a silent Namaste

To everyone you meet

Know the inner prompts

As infinite intelligence

Impersonal

Give up all labels

And grand ideas

Swim in the ocean of love

And not even that

Swimming happens

And it is known

By no-one

Fall silent

As the Namaste

Blooms

Everywhere

Fresh News

Everything you think you know

comes from the past

Let it all go

Bring nothing with you

into this new day

Step into the simplicity

Of here and now

With don't know mind

Open hands

and a willing heart

Like a child

wide-eyed and innocent

Listen within

For the fresh news

that

moment

by

moment

reveals a life of

joy

peace

and serenity.

Beyond All Thought

Beyond all thought

All inherited beliefs

About who and what you are

Lies your true Self

Forever at peace

Filled with joy

Connected to the Wisdom

That spins the planets

Eternally present

Awake

Aware

I'll meet you there

On the pathless path

Together we'll return

To where we never left.

Silence

Silence lies at the root of all things

The ground from which they arise

Here, now, early morning light

Incense-perfumed air

I kneel at the altar of inner silence

Thoughts emerge from

dissolve into

Silence

Words form on page

Breath arises and falls

Birdsong

Contented purr of cats

Peaks of perfection

Being born from

Dying into

An ever-present ocean of silence.

Only God

All I ever wanted was God

It is all you ever were

It is all you are

Eternally

All I ever longed for was God

It was all you were ever given

It is all there is

Unchangingly

Do everything for God

See everyone as God

Trust every action is God

Moving in the world

Surrender

Into the serenity

And silence

Of Self

God within

God without

God everywhere

God everyone

Omnipresent

Omniscient

Love

Everything Is

Everything is as it is

Control is illusion

The wind blows

The sea roars

The sun shines

The cat purrs

The people make war

And also love

Slowly

Inexorably

Eyes open

Breath is noticed

Gratitude arises

Life moves

Everything is as it is

A Dance Of Love

Life moves and moves and moves

Living itself

Moving its manifestations

Breathing its vessels

Gracefully choreographing

A perfect dance of love.

The Sanctuary Of Now

All stories are found in the past

Don't go there

Be present

All judgment is found in the stories

Don't tell them

Be still

Stay here

In quietness

Enjoy the peace and joy

In the sanctuary of now

Don't Forget To Laugh!

Happiness is your true nature

Don't squander it

With the petty judgments

Of the illusory self

Who thinks she knows

Nothing is known

No-one to know

Do you see

The simplicity?

No self-improvement plans

No self to improve

The cosmic joke!

Don't forget to laugh!

I Am That I Am

There is no separation

No me

No you

Boundaries dissolve

Into sparkling light

I am that I am

And there is nothing

And no-one else.

An Endless Namaste

I could withdraw from the world

But I choose to love it

I could retreat into bliss

But I choose to serve

The paradox of awakening

Never for oneself

Always for One Self

As soon as I know I AM

I know you are too

I could sit for endless aeons

In blissful silent joy

But instead

I choose

An endless Namaste

13959560R00083